Growing
Herbs

Growing Herbs

WRITER
ROBERTA FLODEN

PHOTOGRAPHER
SAXON HOLT

LAWN & GARDEN

Product Manager: Cynthia Folland, NK Lawn & Garden Co.

Acquisition, Development and Production Services:
BMR, Corte Madera, CA

Acquisition: Jack Jennings, Bob Dolezal

Series Concept: Bob Dolezal

Project Directors: Jane Ryan, Jill Fox

Developmental Editor: Jill Fox

Horticultural Consultants: Barbara Stremple,
   RG Turner Jr

Photographic Director: Saxon Holt

Art Director (cover): Karryll Nason

Art Director (interior): Brad Greene

Cover Design: Karen Emerson

Cover Photo: Saxon Holt

Photo Assistant: Peggy Henry

Copy Editor: Barbara Ferenstein

Proofreader: Fran Taylor

Typography and Page Layout: Barbara Gelfand

Indexer: Sylvia Coates

Color Separations: Prepress Assembly Incorporated

Printing and Binding: Pendell Printing Inc.

Production Management: Jane Ryan, Brad Greene

Cover: Combine parsley, chives, golden sage, silver thyme,
rosemary and nasturtium in a container for a colorful kitchen
herb garden in a very small space.

First Edition

Library of Congress Cataloging-in-Publication Data:
Floden, Roberta.
   Growing herbs / writer, Roberta Floden ;
   photographer Saxon Holt.
      p. cm.
   Includes index.
   ISBN: 1-880281-13-9
   1. Herb gardening. 2. Herbs. 3. Herbs--Utilization.
I. Title.
 SB351.H5F57 1993
 635.7--dc20   93-20810
                                                        CIP

Special thanks to: Valerie Brown; Luther Burbank Gardens,
Santa Rosa, California; California School for Herbal Studies,
Forestville, California; Fred Caballero and Hilary Langhorst;
Center for Seven Generations Garden, Occidental,
California; French Laundry Restaurant, Yountville,
California; Garden Valley Ranch, Petaluma, California;
Korbel Champagne Cellars, Guerneville, California;
Madrone Manor, Healdsburg, California; Mom's Head
Herbs, Santa Rosa, California; Eleanor Moscow; Betty
Rollins; UC Botanic Gardens, Berkeley, California.

TABLE OF CONTENTS

ENJOYING HERBS

Practical and pretty, herbs offer a multitude of delights. The term *herb* is not a botanical classification but simply refers to a group of plants that are useful to people. Season after season, herbs provide the gardener with decorative foliage and long-lasting flowers, the cook with seasonings for recipes and the creative person with distinctive materials for crafts.

Whether grown in containers or in the ground, herbs are a charming addition to the garden. Many will grow indoors, providing year-round pleasure. Easy-to-grow herbs are a good choice for both the experienced and beginning gardener.

Use culinary herbs for garnishing, for flavoring gourmet vinegars, for mixing into butters, as an alternative to salt for seasoning recipes and for brewing tasty teas.

Many herbs dry easily, retaining their colors and fragrances in long-lasting floral arrangements, in sweet-smelling potpourris and on seasonal wreaths. Home-grown herbs made into craft items make thoughtful gifts.

USING THIS BOOK

Consider this handy volume as three herb books inside one cover. First, this is an alphabetical array of the most popular herbs grown by the home gardener in North America. Each herb is shown in a full-color photograph and identified by both its common and botanical names. Information for each herb includes whether it is an annual or a perennial, its proper propagation method, its sun and soil needs, whether or not it can be grown indoors and specific ideas for landscape uses. Turn to the easy-to-use Herb Reference Chart beginning on page 74 for quick referral.

Of special interest is the lore attached to many herbs. Whenever possible, the origin of the name, the historic uses and the mythology of these herbs are described. These fascinating stories make fun reading and great storytelling. Telling the stories to children will pass the lore on to another generation and may spark an interest in gardening, cooking and craftmaking with herbs.

The second book you hold is a gardener's guide to growing herbs. Informational text and step-by-step instructions, spaced throughout the book, show how and where to use herbs in the home landscape; how to prepare soil for best results; propagation and planting methods; and proper watering, feeding and pest control. Ideas for indoor, outdoor and container gardeners allow you to grow herbs in any climate, throughout the year, no matter how small your yard may be. Use the Index (see page 78) to find a specific topic.

Finally, this is a book filled with ideas for using all the wonderful herbs you've taken such care to grow. Out of the garden, herbs have numerous culinary and craft uses. The preserving and drying methods, herb recipes and craft ideas presented on the following pages show many ways to enjoy herbs.

ANISE
Pimpinella anisum

A LICORICE-FLAVORED ANNUAL

Anise is an aromatic plant, with clusters of white flowers that bloom in early summer and form small, ridged seeds. Anise grows best in a sandy, well-drained soil in full sun and, once established, can survive with a minimum of watering.

Because anise forms a *taproot*—a long slender root that grows deeply downward—it is difficult to transplant. The plant does best when sown directly in the garden after the last frost. If starting anise indoors, use peat pots that can then be placed directly into the soil. Anise seeds take 14 to 18 days to germinate.

Anise is mainly grown for its licorice-flavored and scented seeds. These seeds are used in cakes, cosmetics and liqueurs. Harvest the seedheads when they are gray-green. Wash the seedheads and spread them on a towel to dry. When they are thoroughly dry, rub several seedheads together between your palms and the seeds will fall out.

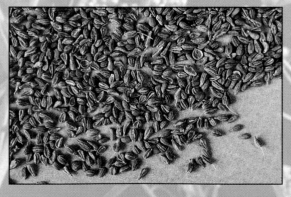

DESIGNING A GARDEN

Flowering plants are either *annuals, biennials* or *perennials*. An annual completes its life cycle in one season. That means it grows from seed, flowers, forms new seed for the next season's growth and dies. Biennials complete their life cycle in two years. The first year they put out green growth and the second year they flower, set seed and die. Perennials are plants that can live more than two years. They often die back into the ground at some point in the year but the roots remain alive and, after a dormant period, send out new growth.

In general, herbs grow best in good, loose, well-drained soil supplied with a moderate amount of organic material and compost in a location that gets between five and six hours of sunshine a day. Grow herbs with similar water and exposure requirements together. A simple plot or raised bed located on the sunniest side of the house is perfect for herbs.

For best results, follow basic landscape design guidelines when planting herb gardens. Place taller plants such as dill and fennel so that they don't shade the shorter herbs such as chives or the sprawling herbs such as thyme. Combine herbs that have contrasting flower and leaf tones and different textures and shapes. Group a selection of herbs with flowers that bloom at the same time for one burst of activity or group those that bloom at different times from spring to fall for months of beautiful garden color.

Make individual beds or use containers for herbs that spread rapidly such as mint. Otherwise these aggressive herbs may eventually take over the yard.

Place markers where you have sown seeds or planted seedlings so you will have no trouble locating and identifying the plants as they grow. Do not plant any food crop in raised beds built of preservative-treated lumber.

BASIL

Ocimum species

Holy Basil

O. sanctum

Holy or sacred basil is revered by the Hindu people who grow it around their temples. It has a musky fragrance similar to cloves. Although some people find its aroma and taste appealing, others find both unpleasant. Use the textured leaves fresh in salads and other cold dishes.

Sweet Basil

O. basilicum

Sweet basil is an important culinary herb, distinguished by its intense flavor and sweet scent. It produces an abundance of large leaves throughout its growing season. Used extensively in salads, tomato dishes and vinegars, sweet basil is the major ingredient in pesto, a flavorful green Italian sauce.

THE KING OF HERBS

Basil is a heat-loving, aromatic annual easily grown from seed. Seeds can be started indoors and the seedlings transplanted or sown outdoors after the last frost when daytime temperatures reach 60° F. Grow basil outdoors in a sunny, protected area in rich, well-drained soil mixed with well-rotted manure or compost, or in containers indoors and out.

Seed germination occurs in about five to seven days. To avoid *damping off,* a fungus growth that can destroy the seedlings, keep the soil evenly but barely moist and allow air to circulate freely. Seedlings can be transplanted after they have four sets of leaves.

Although basil can be grown for its ornamental value, it is most often grown for its flavorful leaves. To encourage fullness and a substantial leaf harvest, pinch and prune basil every two or three weeks. Feeding the plants with a complete fertilizer will also encourage growth, but may alter the flavor of leaves. If flowers are allowed to form, they will set seed and inhibit leaf growth.

To harvest leaves, cut whole branches or sprigs before flower buds open. Most basil leaves can be eaten fresh from the plant or stored via drying, freezing or in oil or vinegar. Oil-stored leaves may blacken, but they will keep their flavor for several months.

The French call basil the *herbe royale*. The Greek name for it means "king." Ancient Greek and Roman physicians thought that a good crop of basil was wrought only if the seed sowing was accompanied by curses and shouts. Thus the French idiom *semer le basilic,* sowing the basil, which means to be raving mad.

Lemon Basil

O. basilicum 'Citriodorum'

With its strong spicy lemon fragrance and tart flavor, lemon basil is an outstanding plant for flavoring food and for adding aroma to the garden. Because it grows compactly, consider planting lemon basil along paths where it can be brushed to release its scent.

Spicy Globe Basil

O. basilicum 'Spicy Globe'

A dwarf variety of sweet basil, spicy globe is a compact, globe-shaped plant with small leaves that makes an excellent container plant and a pretty border plant. The flavor is good and the yellow color and lovely fragrance will add drama to herb vinegars and when used for garnishing.

Dark Opal

O. basilicum 'Dark Opal'

A decorative variety of sweet basil, 'Dark Opal' is cultivated mainly for its colorful purple foliage. It has all the culinary uses of green basil and is a wonderful choice for coloring vinegars, giving them deep pink to red tints.

Thai Basil

O. canum var.

A native of Asia, Thai basil adds an anise-like flavor to many traditional Chinese and Thai dishes. Try it as an exotic touch to any cuisine, including Italian tomato-based dishes, poached pears, baked apples and melon salads.

BAY LAUREL
Laurus nobilis

GROW A VICTORY CROWN

Used by the Greeks and Romans in their victory crowns and garlands—*nobilis* means "renowned"—bay laurel is an evergreen perennial. In cold climates, grow it in a container that can be moved indoors in winter. In temperate climates, it grows easily and can reach a height of 40 feet. Bay laurel has a reputation for being difficult to propagate from seed or cuttings. It may be easier to purchase a small plant from a nursery.

Place bay laurel in a location with rich, well-drained soil and filtered to full sun. In spring, it requires regular watering. Keep it on the dry side for the rest of the year, even if growing it indoors.

Grow bay laurel as a standard, a small tree with a single, strong trunk that can support the foliage head. The leaves are fragrant and shiny. It has clusters of yellow flowers that bloom in early summer, followed by small purplish black berries. Bay laurel responds well to close pruning and is an easy plant to espalier against a wall, shear into a hedge or form into a topiary.

Cut and gather branches in any season for wreaths. The leaves keep their shape, although their dark green color lightens with drying. Pluck leaves at any time to use in recipes where their spicy flavor is desired. Remove leaves before serving because their edges are sharp and should not be swallowed. Place whole fresh leaves in canisters of rice, flour and cereals to serve as insect repellents. Leaves can be dried and stored but lose their pungency. Crumble dried leaves into potpourris and sachets or add them to bathwater for a soothing soak.

Soil Preparation

To prepare soil for growing herbs, start in early spring before planting. Dig the soil to a depth of about one foot and thoroughly clear it of rocks, weeds and debris. Break down solid clods of soil to increase air spaces and improve drainage.

Average garden soil with good drainage and a porous, crumbly texture plus a moderate amount of organic material will usually support a productive herb garden. To provide optimum growing conditions for an individual herb, check its soil requirements on the Herb Reference Chart beginning on page 74.

Improve and enrich the soil by working in organic amendments such as compost, rotted manure, leaf mold, lawn clippings and other humus-building materials. Amendments lighten and aerate heavy clay soil and add organic matter to improve water retention of sandy soil. They will also create an environment in which microorganisms can flourish. Microorganisms break down the organic matter, releasing nutrients the plant roots absorb. Mix the amendments into the soil thoroughly.

Water well and allow the soil to settle after amending and before sowing seeds or planting seedlings. After planting, spread a thin layer of compost over seeds and around transplants.

Once herbs are established, allow them to dry out between waterings. This keeps roots from rotting. Correct drainage problems by adding organic amendments. If the soil is too difficult to correct, consider installing a raised bed filled with improved soil (see page 27) or growing herbs in containers.

For container gardening, use sterilized soil in good condition. Use garden soil only if it has been cleared of weeds and insects and is light enough to allow good drainage in a confining pot. To be sure of clean soil, purchase bags of ready-mixed all-purpose soil.

Neyther falling sickness, neyther devyll, wyll infest or hurt one in that place where a bay tree is.

Thomas Lupton,
Book of Notable Things, 1575

BORAGE
Borago officinalis

A hardy annual, borage has a sprawling habit that blends nicely with wildflowers and vegetables. Sow seeds in the fall or very early spring, placing them approximately 20 inches apart. It doesn't transplant well but reseeds readily. Borage is a particularly beautiful choice for planting on a hill because its cobalt blue flowers tend to nod and dangle. Also called bee-bread, the flowers attract bees all summer long.

Eat borage leaves and flowers fresh; they do not dry well. The flowers are lovely added to fruit salads, floated in punches or frozen in ice cubes. The small, tender leaves add a cucumber taste to salads and sandwiches.

Landscape Ideas

All-Edible Raised Bed

Perfect in a sunny spot near the kitchen door, a small raised bed filled with borage and other culinary herbs provides easy access at a moment's notice. Initially grow three plants each of six favorite herbs with similar water and light needs. Avoid using herbicides, insecticides and preservative-treated lumber near food crops.

Container Plants

Fill containers with colorful herbs to enjoy the lovely flowers indoors and out. Theme container gardens can be fun. Try planting all Asian-native herbs in one container to give your garden a touch of oriental charm; plant commonly used cooking herbs in one container and place it by the kitchen door for easy access.

Path Border

Interplant two or three fragrant herbs along a path. They will give off their scent as people brush past. Combine low- and medium-height herbs with contrasting leaf colors and sizes that have similar growing needs. For a long blooming season, select spring- to fall-blooming herbs. Prune the flowers before they go to seed to control growth the following year.

Formal Garden

The symmetrical patterns of formal gardens look best with neat-growing herbs of contrasting foliage colors and textures. Within the formal layout, planting can be informal, and often the most effective designs are quite simple. Consider circles within circles, a diamond within a rectangle or a rainbow of rows of different-colored flowers.

CARAWAY
Carum carvi

SEEDS FOR SPICING

Caraway is a hardy biennial. In fall or early spring sow seeds directly into the soil in a spot with good drainage and full sun. Allow eight to twelve inches between plants.

In its first year, caraway grows about a foot and puts down a taproot (see page 8). In its second year, clusters of pink or white flowers appear above the foliage, ripening in mid summer into fruit. Each fruit contains two small crescent-shaped seeds.

Timing is important for harvesting seeds (see page 49). To harvest seeds, cut the long stalks to the ground, carefully bundle the stalks together, put them in a paper bag and hang upside down. Let the seeds drop into the bag. After a few weeks, when the seeds are dry, remove them from the bag and store in a covered jar.

Every part of the plant is edible. Use the dried seeds, whole or ground, for baking and when making pickles. Use the leaves for garnishing. The taproot is considered a delectable vegetable. Harvest it after the second year. It can be steamed, pureed or eaten raw, much like a turnip.

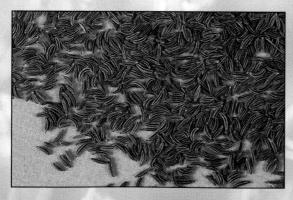

Sowing Seeds Outdoors

First Prepare the soil by digging it deeply, removing weeds and rocks and adding organic amendments (see pg. 13). Water thoroughly and let settle. Create holes or rows to hold seeds. Add a thin layer of mulch, which will help retain moisture, in the hole or furrow.

Third Cover seeds lightly with soil and then firm soil using your hand. Write the date seeds were planted on the seed packet and use it as a marker. Water with a fine spray, keeping soil moist but not wet.

Then Plant 2 or 3 seeds together. Expect to lose some seedlings to insects, birds and weather. Check seed packets for individual depth and spacing instructions for each herb.

Last Thin crowded areas and weaker seedlings by cutting them at the soil line using small scissors (so as not to damage adjacent seedlings). Once 4 leaves have formed on a seedling you can move those herbs that transplant easily to another garden area.

CATNIP
Nepeta cataria

Catnip is a hardy, vigorous, easily grown perennial. A member of the mint family, it prefers sandy, moist soil and sun. Propagate catnip by seeds, stem cuttings or divisions. Catnip reseeds readily. Grow it as a ground cover, cutting it back after flowering so that it remains bushy.

Catnip's aroma has a great attraction for cats, who tend to cavort among and nibble on the seedlings. Because of this, consider growing it in a separate bed and protecting it. The dried leaves can be used for mild teas, but they are mainly sewed into feline toys.

Starting Seeds for Transplant

First Start herb seeds indoors 6–8 weeks before they are to go in the garden. Choose clean, small, 2–4 in.–deep containers with drainage holes such as flats, peat pots, peat pellets or egg cartons.

Third Thoroughly moisten. To retain moisture, cover the containers and trays loosely with plastic with a few holes perforated to allow air circulation. Plastic should not touch the planting medium.

Fifth Once seeds have germinated, place containers in full sun and remove the plastic cover. Start regular watering immediately. Transfer seedlings that have sprouted 4 or more leaves to individual interim 4-in. containers.

Then To avoid diseases and insect pests, use sterilized potting soil or a seed-starter mixture as a planting medium. Place 2 seeds together in small holes or furrows. Check individual seed packets for planting depth. Cover and lightly firm planting medium around the seeds.

Fourth Place containers in a well-lighted place, but avoid full sun. A sunny windowsill or greenhouse window is a good warm place to start seeds. Or place containers under grow lights for a minimum of 12 hours each day.

Last Before planting them in the garden, *harden off* seedlings for a week by placing herbs in a sunny, protected spot outdoors for an hour at first, increasing the exposure by 1 hour daily. Bring them indoors at night.

CHAMOMILE

Chamaemelum species, *Matricaria* species, *Anthemis* species

Chamomile is the common name for several plants, both annual and perennial. They all have aromatic feathery foliage and small daisy-like flowers. All prefer dry, sunny sites. Sow chamomile seeds where they are going to grow, spacing seeds between eight and twelve inches apart. Chamomile reseeds freely. Propagate by dividing mature plants in spring.

Roman chamomile, *Chamaemelum nobile*, is a creeping evergreen perennial that grows four to ten inches high. Because it emits a pleasant aroma when tread upon, use it mainly as a ground cover, around stepping stones or as a lawn substitute. Mow it occasionally to encourage fuller growth.

German Chamomile
Matricaria recutita
This annual chamomile is an easily grown 2 ft.–tall apple-scented herb. Pick the daisy-like flowers in full bloom before they form seed. Dry them to make a soothing, intensely flavored iced or hot tea.

Good Herbs for Tea

Basil	Mints
Bay laurel	Parsley
Borage	Rosemary
Caraway	Sage
Chamomile	Savory
Chives	Scented peppermint
Cilantro	geranium
Dill	Sorrel
Fennel	Tarragon
Lemon verbena	Thyme
Lovage	Watercress
Marjoram	

Dyer's Chamomile
Anthemis tinctoria

Use the golden yellow button flowers of this 3 ft.–high perennial in tea and potpourris. As its name *tinctoria* implies, it yields a yellow dye. A milder tea than German chamomile, it also can be used as a natural hair rinse. Plant divisions in full sun or very light shade. Water moderately.

HERB TEA

Of all the many uses of herbs, one of the most enjoyable is the brewing and drinking of herb tea. The leaves, flowers, seeds and roots of many herbs have been used this way for centuries. A nice advantage of herb teas over conventional teas is that they contain no caffeine. They make a healthful, soothing and refreshing addition to the daily diet and can be served hot or iced.

Make leaf and flower teas by infusing them in the same manner as black tea. Use approximately two to three teaspoons of freshly cut or frozen leaves or flowers, or one teaspoon of dried leaves or flowers, for each six-ounce serving. Put the ingredients into a teapot, pour boiling water over them and steep the mixture for four to five minutes. Strain the tea into a cup. Steeping herbs too long can ruin delicate flavors. Make teas stronger by brewing more ingredients and sweeter by adding honey after brewing.

To brew seed tea, add the seeds to a pot of boiling water and steep for five to ten minutes. To intensify the flavors, crush seeds just before brewing.

For root tea, make a decoction by adding the herb to water and boiling it for 15 to 20 minutes to draw out the fragrant flavor.

Iced tea requires three tablespoons of fresh or two tablespoons of dried herbs. The extra amount allows for the melting ice. Freeze sprigs of herbs such as mint and lovage in ice cubes and add these to black or herb iced teas for decoration.

Herbs have a long history in other beverages besides tea. Rosemary is one of the 130 or more herbs that the Carthusian monks use to flavor chartreuse liqueur. Anise seeds are used in anisette, caraway in Kummel and mint in crème de menthe.

It's important to be certain of the identity of any herb before ingesting it in any manner. Not all herbs are suitable for tea, and some are not recommended for consumption at all.

CHERVIL
Anthriscus derefolium

A delicately flavored hardy annual, chervil thrives in shade and cool weather. It grows best from fresh seed planted in moist, well-drained soil in the fall or early spring. It is also called French parsley and is used in *fines herbes*. Use chervil's anise-flavored leaves generously in salads and soups either fresh, dried or frozen.

Chervil self-sows easily, providing a year-round supply of leaves. To create a bushy plant and keep chervil from becoming leggy, pinch it back by taking the flower stem between thumb and forefinger and removing it above the leaf node, the point on the stem where the leaf appears.

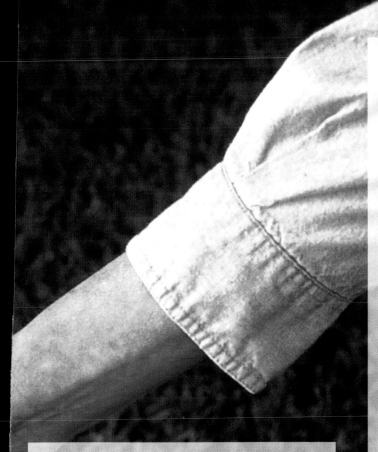

HERB LORE

Herbs are ancient plants, and their history goes back at least 5,000 years. Every human culture has used them to flavor foods as well as for cosmetics, liniments, deodorizers, salves, perfumes, dyes, love potions, embalming fluids, disinfectants and medicines.

Many Greek and Roman sacred rituals incorporated herbs thought to be beloved by their gods. Romans made crowns from bay laurel, used rosemary for temple incense and draped sacred animals in fragrant herbs for sacrifice. In Greek mythology, Minthe was a nymph whom Pluto transformed into the herb because of his wife's jealousy.

The Romans valued herbs so highly that they took seeds of some 200 kinds—including fennel, sage, parsley, rosemary, thyme and borage—with them to cultivate when exploring new lands.

On the practical side, Romans spread aromatic *strewing herbs,* such as tansy, mint and thyme, on their floors to mask household odors and to repel pests. Lavender got its name—derived from the Latin *lavare,* to bathe—because it was used frequently in Roman baths.

The Bible suggests that cumin and anise seeds were used as currency. Chervil, purported to have blood- and skin-cleansing qualities, was eaten in quantity during Lent. Hyssop was thought to purify the body of disease and the soul of sin. Bitter herbs— probably tansy at one time and parsley today—are eaten during the Jewish Passover holiday still.

The Chinese thought that cilantro could make a person immortal and developed several recipes with this in mind. In the Arabian tales, *The Thousand and One Nights,* cilantro is said to arouse passion.

Traditional Symbolic Meanings

Basil = Love
Bay = Fame
Chamomile = Wisdom
Chervil = Sincerity
Chives = Usefulness
Dill = Good cheer, Survival
Fennel = Grief, Endurance
Scented Geranium = Happiness
Lavender = Devotion
Marjoram = Joy
Mint = Refreshment
Parsley = Merriment
Rosemary = Remembrance
Sage = Wisdom
Santolina = Virtue
Savory = Interest
Sweet Woodruff = Humility
Tansy = Hostility
Tarragon = Permanence
Thyme = Daring

CHIVES
Allium schoenoprasum

PERENNIAL FLAVOR

Like other onions, chives grow from perennial bulbs. The plant is grown for its hollow slender leaves and its small lavender flowers, both of which are decorative and edible.

Chives can be started from seeds, but they germinate very slowly, requiring darkness, constant moisture and a temperature above 60° F. You can also purchase small plants and transplant them, or obtain a division from another plant. A clump of six to eight bulbs planted in a sunny site will produce leaves and flowers for many years.

Chives grow well in almost any garden setting. Use them as a low-growing border plant or as an edging in herb, flower and vegetable gardens.

Chives are evergreen in mild climates. In cold climates, either grow them in containers year-round or dig up a clump in late summer and plant it in a container for winter use.

The plants maintain a neat appearance even when periodically clipped for kitchen use. To harvest chives, snip out half the leaves at ground level after they are at least six inches tall. Allow the other half to keep growing. Leaf flavor is best right before blossoms appear.

Native to Europe and Asia, chives have been added to foods for nearly 5,000 years. Leaves and flowers of chives should be used fresh. Add either or both to salads, potato dishes and herb vinegars or use them for garnishing. They can be dried, freeze-dried or frozen, but both leaves and flowers lose flavor in storage. The leaves and flowers dry well and can be added to dried arrangements.

Dividing Plants

First To unearth clumps of perennial bulbs such as chives and other plants that spread by runners, moisten the soil well and dig carefully around the plant. This is best done in spring or late summer.

Next To divide the plant, pull apart clusters of independently rooted sections called divisions. Some plants may need to be cut apart. Discard any dead or dying sections.

Last Plant the divisions in newly dug holes before the roots dry out and well before the first frost. Divisions need time to develop new root systems before the ground freezes. Water the divisions well until established.

CILANTRO
Coriandrum sativum

A THREE-FOR-ONE PLANT

Cilantro is a hardy annual grown for its edible leaves, seeds and roots. The delicate parsley-like foliage—the plant is also called Chinese parsley—has a pungent aroma and a lemony-sage flavor. The leaves are a major seasoning in Asian, Latin American and Mediterranean recipes. The aromatic seeds, called coriander, are a very popular ground spice. The taproot, which tastes much like the leaves, can be eaten fresh, chopped or minced in soups and stews or made into tea.

Grow cilantro in spring from seed sown directly in the soil. Cilantro has a taproot and should not be transplanted. Find a location protected from the wind, since cilantro can become topheavy and blow over. For abundant leaves, select a partly shady, moist area.

Leaves can be cut when the plant is approximately five inches tall. Remove the flower heads to stimulate further leaf growth. Over-fertilizing produces a less flavorful plant.

For more coriander seeds, plant in full sun. Harvest the seeds when they turn a fawn color in mid summer to early fall. The plant will reseed if left alone.

Building a Raised Bed

First A raised bed aids in weed and pest control and can be used to separate garden areas. Determine the size of the bed, assemble materials, mark off the area and dig a 2 in.–wide perimeter trench.

Third Loosen the existing soil and work organic amendments into it (see pg. 13). Water thoroughly. Add a mix of soil and organic matter to fill the bed. Water again.

Then Place boards in the trench. Drive support stakes into the ground on both sides of the boards every 16 in. Using lag screws, attach all the corners and the stakes to the boards. Add copper sheeting to the top edges of the boards to deter snails and slugs.

Last Rake the bed, select desired herbs and sow seeds or plant transplants. Cover the bed with flexible netting to protect seeds and plants from birds and cats.

Materials

Stakes and string for marking

Shovel or spade

2 x 12 lumber, cut to desired length

Support stakes

Lag screws

Flexible netting

Copper sheeting

CAUTION

Use redwood or cedar, never preservative-treated lumber, for beds in which food will be grown.

27

CRESSES

Lepidium sativum, Nasturtium officinale, Barbarea verna

Several plants are known by the common name cress. All are easy to grow indoors or in shady spots outdoors. Sow seeds in fall where winters are mild or in very early spring elsewhere. Cresses mature rapidly, but only their thinnings and tender young leaves should be eaten; older leaves have a very strong flavor. Cresses are the oldest known cultivated green vegetable.

Peppergrass, *Lepidium sativum,* is an annual also known as curly cress. Sow seeds in a rich, moist soil in containers. Peppergrass grows indoors or outdoors. The sprouts should be ready to eat in less than two weeks. Use its crisp young leaves in sandwiches and salads or for garnishing.

Watercress, *Nasturtium officinale,* a creeping perennial, grows naturally in running streams, but it can grow in pots of soil placed in tubs of water. Change the water weekly. Sprigs root easily. Use watercress fresh or mix into a herb butter (see pg. 63).

Winter cress, *Barbarea verna,* sometimes called upland cress, broadleaf cress or creasy greens, is a biennial. It flourishes in moist soil in containers both indoors and out. It has a peppery flavor and can be used in the same manner as the other cresses.

GROWING HERBS INDOORS

An indoor herb garden provides interesting greenery, instant flavorings for foods and lovely fragrance to rooms. It takes somewhat different gardening techniques to keep indoor plants healthy, but it can be done. Most herbs will thrive if sufficient light, air circulation and moisture are supplied. Note that herbs grown indoors may not be as fragrant or taste as good as those grown outdoors and may be vulnerable to pest problems and diseases.

It is important that herbs be planted in clean clay, plastic or ceramic containers. Group several herbs with similar water and light requirements together in medium- to large-sized containers. Keep in mind the design principles of color, texture, forms of leaves and time of bloom when grouping plants.

When selecting herbs for an indoor garden, choose those that can be grown from seeds in containers, that have compact growth patterns and that have a branching root system rather than a taproot.

Grow herbs in very bright south- or west-facing windows that receive at least five hours of sunlight a day. When natural light is unavailable, use fluorescent lights that aid plant growth to keep the plants productive and bushy. Place the lights just above the plants and be prepared to raise the fixture as the plants grow.

To provide adequate air circulation, leave space between containers. To increase humidity, place the pots on trays of moist gravel or pebbles. To ensure healthy herbs indoors, spray the leaves with room temperature, unsoftened water occasionally (to keep dust from collecting on the leaves). Apply half-strength liquid fertilizer regularly and harvest less than a quarter of a plant at one time.

Use these distinctive plants for decoration around the house, but remember to return the herb to its sunny spot for best growth.

DILL
Anethum graveolens

A BEWITCHING INGREDIENT

Dill is a self-seeding, bee-attracting annual. Each plant is a single stem, about three feet tall, with aromatic leaves and flavorful seeds. It makes an attractive backdrop along a garden perimeter. Sow the seeds in early spring directly into a sunny, well-drained spot as dill forms a taproot that does not transplant well.

Once the plant is established, harvest the leaves by snipping close to the stem. Harvested leaves lose their strong flavor after a couple of days. Dill can be dried. For a steady supply, freeze the stalk together with the leaves and snip the leaves as needed.

Two or three weeks after the flowers blossom, harvest the light brown seeds in the same manner as caraway (see page 16). Use seeds in vinegars and as a pickling spice.

The name comes from the Norse *dilla*, which means *to lull;* dill was once used to induce relaxation and sleep. Some people hang branches of dill above doors as a charm against witches.

GARNISHING WITH HERBS

Herbs enhance the entire dining experience when used to decorate dishes. For garnishing, choose edible leaves or flowers without blemishes.

Fresh cut herbs—from garden or market—will keep for several days if stored properly. Place stem ends in a vase of cold water, in the same manner as fresh flowers.

Herb garnishes should be used to enhance the meal, not merely to fill up the plate. These are some traditional combinations:

- Basil leaves on fruit and cottage cheese
- Borage flowers candied on cakes, cookies and fruit salads
- Chervil on rice and mixed in cream cheese for spreading on bagels
- Chive flowers on potato dishes
- Dill in sour cream for a quick chip dip
- Lemon verbena floated in teas
- Lovage seeds sprinkled over bread
- Mint leaves in melon or grain salads or frozen in ice cubes and added to summer drinks
- Parsley on smoked salmon, breads or rice
- Scented geranium leaves as decoration for jellies, puddings, cakes and cookies
- Tarragon shredded onto pears

SEASONING BLENDS

Blends of ground herbs are another useful, flavorful addition to the table. Herb blends can be salt-free or contain varying quantities of salt. Salt-free blends are particularly appealing for people on low-sodium diets.

For seasoned salt, combine one cup of noniodized kosher or sea salt to one cup of fresh herbs (five to eight tablespoons dry herbs). Crush the herb leaves with the salt in a mortar and pestle, or mix them in a blender. If using fresh herbs, place the mixture on a baking sheet in a 200° F oven for about an hour and let cool before storing. Store herb blends in air-tight jars. They will keep for about a year.

FENNEL
Foeniculum vulgare

Fennel is a semi-hardy perennial grown for its filigreed leaves and attractive flowers. The entire plant—leaves, flowers, seeds and stems—is edible. Plant fennel seeds in the fall. A plant steeped in mythology, fennel was used by Prometheus to bring fire to humans.

Because of its 4–6 ft. height, bronze fennel, *F. vulgare* 'Rubrum', makes a good background plant. It produces edible copper, pink and bronze leaves that add thick plumes and a rich color accent to the spring garden.

Common Fennel

F. vulgare

Common, also known as sweet or wild, fennel is a perennial often grown as a summer annual. It is drought-tolerant and tends to naturalize in warmer climates. The leaves taste like sweet licorice. They don't dry well because heat destroys their flavor. Use the leaves fresh in salads and soups. Grind the seeds to flavor baked goods.

Florence Fennel

F. vulgare var. *azoricum*

Florence fennel or Finocchio has similar growing habits to other fennels. Its large celery-like stems have an edible swollen leaf base that can be eaten fresh or, for a mellower flavor, steamed or baked.

The fennel with its yellow flowers,
In an earlier age than ours,
Was gifted with the wondrous powers
Lost vision to restore.

Henry Wadsworth Longfellow

HYSSOP
Hyssopus officinalis

A compact, winter-hardy evergreen perennial, hyssop is a member of the mint family with a camphor-like medicinal aroma. It is easy to grow in containers or in the ground in light, well-drained soil and full sun. Hyssop is rarely bothered by pests, disease or lack of moisture. Propagate by seed, cuttings or division. Bees, butterflies and hummingbirds are attracted to its sweet-scented flowers.

Hyssop is a lovely plant that deserves a prominent place in the garden. To keep it bushy, frequently clip it to 6 in. tall. Hyssop is a favorite plant to edge a formal herb or knot garden. In less formal plantings, it makes a nice border combined with feathery herbs such as dill and anise.

Transplanting Herbs Outside

First Water and harden off plants in advance (see pg. 19). Space plants with room to grow. Using a trowel, dig holes as needed in soil that is cleared, prepared and watered (see pg. 13). Dig holes larger than the rootball. Transplant on a cloudy day for least shock.

Third Place the plant into the hole up to its first true leaves—those leaves that have the characteristics of the mature herb. Fill the hole halfway with soil, pressing it around the roots. Water. Fill hole with soil.

Then Holding the plant between your fingers, turn the container over. Tap the bottom and the sides of the pot gently until the roots are free. Carefully ease the plant out; try to maintain soil around roots.

Last Water the soil gently but well. Avoid splashing soil onto the leaves. Make sure stalks remain upright. On a plant marker, identify the herb, write the date, and leave space to track fertilizing, trimming and harvesting times.

LAVENDER
Lavandula species

English Lavender
L. angustifolia
Probably one of the most aromatic examples of the species, English lavender is hardy, grows to 3 ft. tall and is woody. Planted in a well-drained, sunny location, it will produce an abundance of flower spikes. Once established, it will live indefinitely.

French Lavender
L. dentata
The fragrant flowers of French lavender bloom almost continually in mild, sunny climates. Its special quality is its fern-like leaves. A good container plant, it can be grown indoors year-round in a sunny window or grown outdoors most of the year and moved indoors in winter.

FRAGRANCE OF DEVOTION

Lavender is one of the best-loved herbs. Traditionally known as the herb of devotion, its flowers hold one of the finest fragrances in nature. A small evergreen perennial shrub, it has many varieties, each with very aromatic flower spikes in shades of purple, blue, white or pink. Propagate lavender by seed or cuttings. Take cuttings from side shoots that appear in summer.

With its delicate flowers and silver-gray, fine-textured foliage, lavender looks especially dramatic against plants with contrasting dark green leaves. Plant it next to walks or paths, along borders, in rock gardens, in containers or as a hedge. It will perfume a garden and attract bees, but deer will not touch it.

The plants like full sun and well-drained soil. For a compact plant and the best perfume, grow plants in sandy or gravelly soil, let them dry completely between waterings and do not fertilize.

The entire plant is fragrant, but the flowers have the strongest scent. Cut flowers when the perfume oils are most concentrated—on hot afternoons when the flowers are just beginning to open. Harvest leaves at any time.

After flowering, either remove the flower spikes or cut back the plant so it doesn't become leggy. Prune lavender in spring to encourage new, soft growth.

Use flowers to flavor jams or crystallized for garnishing. Craft uses include making lavender sticks.

Historically the edible but bitter lavender flowers were used medicinally to aid sore throats and hoarseness, to help heal cuts, burns and stings and as a strewing herb.

Spike Lavender

L. latifolia

Looking much like English lavender and often confused with it, spike lavender has flower stalks that are branched and leaves that are broader than the English variety. This is the most common lavender for commercial use.

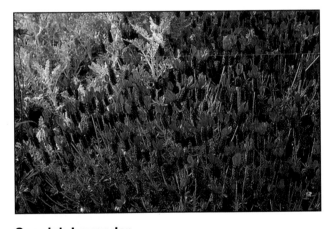

Spanish Lavender

L. stoechas

The dark purple flowers of Spanish lavender bloom in early spring on tight, short spikes. Its leaves have a gray cast. It is more delicate than other lavenders and must be brought indoors or otherwise protected in winter. It makes a charming container plant.

Making Lavender Sticks

First Harvest 10–15 flower spikes, leaving a long stem on each one. The higher buds on each spike should just be opening. Strip the lower leaves from each stem, fit the flower heads together and trim the ends of the stems evenly.

Last Using narrow string or thread, bind each bundle together just under the lowest flowers. Wrap ribbon around stems and tie. Add decorative ribbons and bows. Store by hanging flower-end down. Use lavender sticks to decorate baskets, wreaths and gift boxes or as a sachet.

LEMON VERBENA
Aloysia triphylla

Lemon verbena is a tender perennial. In cold climates grow it as an annual, plant it indoors in containers or dig it up in fall and store it indoors in moist sand in a cool, dark place and replant in spring. Lemon verbena likes full sun and rich, sandy, well-drained soil. Fertilize it at planting time.

Use the pinched growing tips and fresh leaves of lemon verbena for tea and in fruit salad or custard pudding. Add them to finger bowls for an elegant touch on the dining table. Dry them for potpourris and sachets. Lemon verbena is the only lemon-scented herb that retains its full scent even after drying.

To keep herb plants dense and shapely, pinch off growing tips to force lateral growth. Lemon verbena tends to be leggy and responds well to pinching.

Watering and Fertilizing

Watering and fertilizing all herbs at once on an arbitrary schedule may give too much to one herb yet not enough for its neighbor to survive. The most effective schedule is to observe individual plants and give them what they require when they require it. Track fertilizing times on the plant marker.

For most herbs, one half-strength fertilizer feeding at planting—or at the beginning of the growing season for established plants—is enough. Organic matter—compost, rotted manure or leaf mold—improves drainage and air circulation in heavy clay soils and helps retain moisture and nutrients in light sandy soils. Add a balanced fertilizer that contains nitrogen for green leaves, phosphorous for flowers and growth and potash for roots. Follow the label directions carefully. Herbs established in good soil may not need any additional nutrients. In richly fertilized soils, herb plants will be lush and attractive, but weak in fragrance and flavor.

Once established, herbs often thrive on limited amounts of water. An essential requirement for most herbs is well-drained soil, as water remaining near the roots can foster rot. Thin, sandy soils drain faster than heavy clay soils. In general, over-watering is more of a problem to herbs than under-watering. When watering, water thoroughly to develop a deep, strong root system.

For herbs that require dry soil, allow the ground to dry completely between waterings. For herbs that prefer average moisture, water as soon as the surface of the soil is dry. For those that require abundant moisture, keep the soil evenly moist.

Each spring add mulch around the base of each herb plant. The best mulch choices are rice hulls, straw and compost. Commercial mulches are available. Mulch keeps roots moist, decreases their water need and helps maintain soil moisture and temperature levels.

LOVAGE
Levisticum officinale

Lovage is a hardy perennial that prefers a moist, rich soil. It requires filtered summer sun and freezing winter temperatures to ensure growth in spring. Propagate by seed in fall or by division in spring or fall. Because it grows to be almost six feet tall and just about as wide, lovage is an ideal plant for a shady spot in the back of the garden.

The taste of lovage resembles a very pungent celery. Use the tender leaves and aromatic seeds fresh or dried in salads, soups and stews. It can, in fact, replace celery in recipes.

CONTROLLING PESTS

For centuries, certain herbs have been known to repel pests. In the past, strewing herbs—those known to repel ants, flies, fleas and mice—were spread inside the house to keep infestations at bay. Although today it is uncommon to strew herbs on floors, it is common to place bundles of dried herbs in drawers and in closets to repel moths and herb containers near entrances to repel ants and flies.

While some herbs serve as pest repellents, some pests must be repelled from herbs. Infestations are a fact of gardening life. Identifying problems early will keep them to a minimum. Routinely inspect leaves and flowers. Twisted or stunted growth, deformed leaves, leaf spots, wilting or root rot are probably caused by fungi or bacteria. Yellow leaves or misshapen growing tips might be due to sap-sucking insects such as aphids, spider mites, whiteflies, thrips or scale. Aphids and scale produce a sticky dew that attracts ants. Leafchewing beetles and larva consume leaves or make tunnels within the leaves.

Good gardening practices prevent most problems. Maintain open space between plants to inhibit insects from spreading. Put copper sheeting around garden beds to deter snails and slugs. From time to time, use a forceful spray of water to dislodge insects and larvae. Pick off larger pests and destroy them. Wash your hands and tools after dealing with an infested plant to reduce spread. Clean up plant debris to limit opportunities for nesting. Do not compost infested or diseased debris.

If problems are out of control, take measures immediately. Choose natural plant insecticides such as pyrethrum and rotenone for their relative safety for the user and environment. If you must use chemicals, follow label directions carefully.

MINT

Mentha species

Mints are hardy perennials that can grow almost anywhere, but do best in moist, rich soil in partial shade. Mints propagate by *runners,* also called *rhizomes,* underground stems, which can invade the surrounding garden. To control the runners, mints are best planted in containers or in separate beds. Use mint leaves in air fresheners, potpourris, teas and salads and for garnishing.

Bergamot Mint

M. x *piperita* var. *citrata*

The smooth, purple-tinged leaves and purple stems of bergamot have a distinct citrus scent and flavor when crushed. The leaves make a refreshing tea and can be used in colognes, potpourris and sachets.

Apple Mint

M. *suaveolens*

Apple or woolly mint is round-leaved and covered with fuzzy hairs. Its fruity aroma makes it a fragrant ground cover. It can be successfully grown in difficult areas, and its season lasts longer into winter than other mints. It is sweeter and more mellow than other varieties.

Corsican Mint

M. *requienii*

Corsican mint has a rich traditional mint flavor and fragrance, similar to peppermint. Because of its tiny, bright green leaves, miniature flowers and creeping stems, it grows well between paving stones where it scents the air when stepped upon. It must be kept moist.

Peppermint

M. x piperita

Peppermint is a common flavoring for pharmaceuticals, liqueurs and candies. Use peppermint for mint sauce, with chocolate in desserts and for garnishing. Its tea, which is helpful to digestion, can be made from fresh or dried leaves. Crystallize leaves for cake and candy decorations.

Spearmint

M. spicata

A low-growing mint, spearmint has bright green, closely set, toothed leaves with no leaf stalks. It is the most commonly grown mint and is used for tea and flavoring. It is the key ingredient for mint sauces and jelly served with roast lamb.

Pineapple Mint

M. suaveolens 'Variegata'

A decorative form of apple mint, pineapple mint has variegated dappled green and white leaves. It makes a refreshing fruit-flavored tea and is pretty when used for garnishing. Use the dried leaves in sachets and potpourris.

Pennyroyal

M. pulegium

Pennyroyal has a creeping habit and can be used to form a ground cover or lawn substitute, especially in shady situations. Very strong in mint aroma, use it as an insect repellent. Eating pennyroyal is not advised.

NASTURTIUM
Tropaeolum majus

COMPLETELY EDIBLE

Nasturtium is an ornamental annual, which makes a colorful addition to gardens and salads. It is lovely massed in gardens, climbing up trellises, covering hillsides or spilling out of containers. Both the leaves and flowers can be eaten.

Nasturtium will grow in almost any environment as long as the soil is well drained. Start seeds in fall in warm climates and after the last frost in colder areas. They will germinate in about a week, indoors or outdoors, in sun or light shade, in dry or damp soil. The richer and more moist the soil, the more lush the foliage. However, poor soil will garner more flowers and seeds. Nasturtium grow best where nighttime temperatures are cool.

Nasturtium flowers—whose jewel colors run the gamut from white to yellow to salmon to maroon and purple shades—bloom continuously from early summer until the first frost. The flower pods encase three seeds that will reseed. Reseeded plants do not always produce the same color flowers.

Harvest leaves and flowers any time. Use the foliage and flowers fresh in salads or mix them into herb butter (see page 63).

CONTAINER GARDENING

Because they are adaptable and easy to grow, many herbs do very well as container plants. Depending on personal taste, almost any pot, tub, basket or cylinder can be used as a plant container as long as it has drainage. Avoid containers painted with lead paint and any made from wood that has been treated with preservatives. Because clay absorbs moisture, watering needs are greater in clay pots than in plastic or wood.

The decorative possibilities of containers are endless. Be sure that herbs planted together have similar soil, sun and moisture requirements.

Most herbs can be grown in containers; only those that produce a taproot will not be successful. Herbs in containers have the same requirements of light, well-drained soil, nutrients and water as those grown in the ground; the difference is the limited space. Fill the container with sterilized soil (see page 13). Fertilize in approximately one month. Because the soil in containers is quickly drained of both water and nutrients—and roots can't ramble underground in search of them—keep a close eye on water and fertilizer needs.

In the confinement of containers, herbs adapt by growing a bit more slowly and maintaining a smaller size than when grown in the ground. To encourage bushy growth, prune and pinch back herbs often. Roots protruding from the drainage hole indicate the need for a larger container.

OREGANO AND MARJORAM
Origanum species

Common Oregano
O. vulgare
Common oregano, often called wild marjoram, spreads by runners, making it a good choice for a ground cover. Historically this species was used for medicinal purposes. Now, use it in the kitchen for pizza and Italian dishes.

AN HERB BY TWO NAMES

Origanum plants are aromatic, herbaceous perennials native to the Mediterranean. They are known by two common names, marjoram and oregano. All varieties grow in shallow, well-drained soil, in full sun, and emit a spicy fragrance during the summer months. They also are similar in appearance, with small sometimes mottled green leaves and small white or pink flowers that form clusters.

Propagate by seed, cutting or division. Seeds are small and slow to germinate. Start them indoors and transplant them outdoors when all danger of frost is over. Plant them in full sun in light, well-drained soil. They also grow well indoors in a sunny window.

To keep plants thick and lush, pinch new growth frequently. Harvest leaves just before the plant blooms, when leaves are the sweetest. Cut branches to one inch above the ground. In warmer climates, the plants may bloom twice in a season; get a second harvest by cutting to the lowest set of leaves. In cooler climates, a second cutting can weaken the plant.

Use oregano and marjoram sprigs fresh in salads, bath water and closets. Make teas, potpourris and sachets from dried leaves.

The name oregano is from the Greek *oros* and *ganos*, meaning mountain joy, referring to the appearance of the wild varieties on otherwise barren hillsides. In ancient Rome and Greece, marjoram was a symbol of happiness and newly married couples were crowned with it.

Crete Dittany
O. dictamnus
A variation of sweet marjoram grown chiefly as a decorative annual, this tender perennial produces small pretty mounds and purple flowers. It is propagated by cuttings and grows well in containers. The leaves maintain their color and mild flavor when dried for culinary use.

Italian Oregano

O. vulgare subspecies *hirtum*

One of the best tasting of the species, propagate Italian oregano from a root division in spring or a cutting in fall from a plant that you have tasted to ensure its flavor. Enjoy its mellow, pungent taste in Mediterranean dishes.

Golden Oregano

O. vulgare 'Aureum'

With its green and gold variegated leaves, this very attractive form of marjoram is useful in the landscape. Because of its unusual colors, it is a lovely plant to combine in an herb garden container. Grown as an annual, it produces runners that spread rapidly. The leaves are vulnerable to scorching in full sun.

Sweet Marjoram

O. majorana

Sweet marjoram is easily grown from seed. Its beautiful flowers make interesting additions to winter bouquets. Grow this tender perennial outdoors as an annual, transfer it to containers and bring it indoors in winter. Use fresh in recipes and tea. Spicy yet mild, this is the best marjoram for cooking.

Pot Marjoram

O. onites

Also known as Cretan oregano, pot marjoram is a tender perennial that grows to 1 ft. It has dark green, textured leaves and produces small clusters of flowers that bees find quite attractive. Propagate from cuttings. Use fresh leaves for garnishing. Use fresh or dried leaves in salads and teas. Dry the leaves and flowers for potpourri.

PARSLEY
Petroselinum crispum

NOT JUST A GARNISH

Although classified as a biennial, parsley grows best as an annual. If you allow it to grow into its second year, you'll reap flowers and seeds, but little foliage, and what there is will be bitter and tough.

Parsley seeds take almost a month to germinate. Speed things along by soaking the seeds for 24 hours in warm water prior to planting. Because parsley sometimes doesn't transplant well, results are better if seeds sown in the spring are placed directly in the spot the plants are to grow.

Help space parsley's fine seeds by mixing them with sand or dry coffee grounds before sowing. Keep the seed bed evenly moist with gentle spraying while waiting for germination. Grow in full sun to partial shade in moderately rich, moist and well-drained soil. Feed with a high-nitrogen fertilizer such as fish emulsion in spring and after major cuttings. Late summer seeding in a protected spot may produce a late autumn crop.

As an attractive, bright green, compact plant, parsley has a place as a border or edging in both herb and flower gardens. It also grows well in containers, indoors and out. Parsley is winter-hardy in mild climates.

During a season, a mature plant can produce up to one cup of fresh leaves every three weeks. To keep the plants producing leaves, keep the soil moist, fertilize monthly, cut back the outside stems frequently and remove the stalks before they flower.

Parsley contains significant amounts of vitamins A and C, the minerals calcium and iron, and breath-sweetening chlorophyll.

Curly-leafed parsley, *P.c.* var. *crispum,* is prettier in the garden, in containers and for garnishing than flat-leafed species. It makes an excellent herb butter and freezes better than Italian parsley.

The slightly stronger, more pungent flavor of Italian parsley, *P.c.* var. *neapolitanum,* makes it preferable to curly-leafed parsley when it is chopped fresh over eggs, potatoes, rice or pasta and in many slow-cooked recipes. It is the better variety for drying.

To harvest parsley, pick the leaves fresh as needed during the first year. Dry leaves for later use and store them in airtight containers. Collect seeds when ripe. If grown as a biennial, dig up roots and discard in the autumn of the second year.

HARVESTING

In general, harvest only the herbs you need and handle what you cut as little as possible so that volatile oils are not released. Take only the part of the plant required. Gather herbs after the dew has cleared on a dry day. For flavor, harvest leaves before noon; for fragrance, harvest after noon when oils are most pungent. Move the cuttings out of the sun as soon as possible to protect them. If you gather several herbs, keep each type separate to avoid mixing flavors and aromatic oils.

Herbs that send up slender grass-like spears directly from roots—chives, lovage, parsley—require that whole spears be cut. Cut just above the ground level from the outside of the plant so you won't leave unsightly stubble or yellowing leaf tips.

For immediate culinary use, cut fresh sprigs or pinch back tender young tips of herbs at any time during the growing season. Snip annuals a few inches above the ground so that some leaves remain to give energy for continued growth. Pinch perennials a few inches off the tip of each branch. This process promotes new growth and shapeliness.

For drying annual herbs, cut the entire plant unless a second harvest is possible or seeds are desirable. For drying perennial herbs, leave one third or more of the plant. To protect essential oils in flowers to be dried, cut them below the blossom just before or as soon as they open when they are at their best.

To collect seed for kitchen use or for planting during the next season, timing is important. Wait until the seedheads have become dry and the seeds themselves are mature and have lost their green color, about one month after flowers appear. All seeds are harvested in the same manner as caraway (see page 16).

In autumn, harvest roots and bulbs when the top growth has died down and they have the maximum amount of stored food. Dig them up for fresh or dried use.

ROQUETTE
Eruca vesicaria subspecies *sativa*

Roquette, an annual, is also known as arugula, rugula or rocket-salad. It is a gourmet Old World green with a peppery taste similar to watercress. The flavor is best when leaves are young and tender. Harvest the entire plant at ground level or pick the rapidly growing leaves individually and add them to salads.

COOKING WITH HERBS

Herbs add zest to almost all cooked and uncooked dishes. If your experience cooking with herbs involves only using commercially available dried herbs, the use of fresh home-grown herbs will revolutionize your recipes.

Use three to four times the amount of fresh as dried herbs called for in a recipe, depending on the flavor desired. Activate the flavor of dried herbs by soaking them for up to 15 minutes in stocks, lemon juice or dressings or sauteeing them gently in butter or oil before adding to recipes. To achieve the fullest aroma from fresh leaves, rub them between your hands before adding them to recipes.

Add the stronger flavored herbs with some restraint during the last ten minutes of soups and stews; the lighter, milder tasting herbs can be added at the last minute. Rub herbs into meat and chicken before cooking. Season vegetables, fish, eggs and bread with herb butter (see page 63). For soups, add one well-chosen fresh herb for contrast in flavor and color right before serving. Herb seasoning blends make a good substitute for salt in low-sodium diets (see page 31).

Many herb flowers are edible. They make beautiful additions to the table, adding color and perfume to your recipes.

Classic herb combinations are often called for in recipe ingredient lists. *Bouquet garni* is fresh or dried sprigs of thyme, marjoram, bay laurel and parsley, among other aromatic herbs, wrapped or tied in bundles and used in long-simmering foods. Remove the bouquet before serving.

Fines herbes is a combination of chervil, parsley, thyme and tarragon, freshly minced and stirred into or sprinkled on top of cold dishes. Add *fines herbes* to recipes at the very last minute of cooking. Use them with eggs, sautés and cheese sauces.

Roquette grows easily in cool, shady, moist conditions. Sow seeds frequently and in succession directly in the ground for a constant supply from early spring to fall. Harvest the entire plant before the flowers form.

ROSEMARY
Rosmarinus species

HERB OF REMEMBRANCE

A perennial evergreen shrub, rosemary grows well in full sun in average, well-drained soil. It can be grown from seed but is more easily started from cuttings. Rosemary is winter-hardy to 10° F. In colder climates, plant it in a container and bring it indoors when frost arrives. The Latin name *ros marinus* translates as dew of the sea, referring to its growth on the Mediterranean headlands.

The shrub variety, *R. officinalis,* can be pruned into a hedge or stand by itself as an accent plant. The low-growing, dwarf *R. prostratus* works well as a ground cover or in hanging planters.

Pinch new growth and harvest sprigs throughout the year. Use flowering branches in fresh arrangements and for garnishing. Dry the leaves for seasoning recipes and making teas.

Rosemary has a long record in legend. In Shakespeare's *Hamlet,* Ophelia dubs it the herb of remembrance and fidelity. Traditional bridal bouquets are woven with rosemary sprigs to signify love and fidelity.

Taking Cuttings

First Clip a 3–5 in. sprig of strong new growth from the top of the plant just below a leaf. Strip the stem of its bottom leaves leaving 1–2 in. of bare stem and 3–5 leaves.

Then Dip the stem end in water and then in a powdered rooting hormone, which aids in the development of roots. Make sure that the powder sticks to the stem.

Third Prepare a soil mixture of perlite, vermiculite and peat moss, or clean sand. Wet the mixture and place it in a growing flat, container or jar. Place each cutting up to its leaves in the mixture. Space cuttings approximately 2 in. apart.

Fourth Place the flat in a warm spot—with light but not in direct sunlight—or on a safety-approved plant warmer. Loosely cover the flat with a plastic tent in which holes have been punched to retain humidity yet let air circulate. Keep moist.

Fifth Fill interim 4-in. plastic or clay containers with moist, commercial potting soil. Once roots form on cuttings, usually within 6 weeks, transfer cuttings to interim containers.

Last Harden off (see pg. 19) rooted cuttings for 2 weeks to acclimate them to the outdoor climate. When new leaves appear, transplant herbs to selected garden location.

SAGE
Salvia species

THE WISE HERB

Sage is a tough, undemanding perennial and a prolific bloomer. It prefers full sun and sandy, well-drained soil. There are dozens of species, varieties and cultivars, many of which have decorative variegated leaves and spikes of colorful flowers that attract bees and hummingbirds.

Sage is grown easily from seed sown indoors in spring and transplanted outdoors when the weather warms up, but it takes several years to grow a good-sized plant from seed. Propagate by division or cuttings from an established plant. Occasionally prune or pinch the growing tips to keep it compact and bushy. Because of its tendency to get woody and less productive, divide or replace the entire plant every four or five years.

Sage works well in beds, borders and edgings and containers, indoors and out. Sage is generally drought-tolerant.

Species that are not winter-hardy can be grown as low-maintenance annuals. If grown as a perennial, keep the soil quite dry in winter. In spring divide the plant, cut it back and fertilize.

Fresh sage has a strong lemony, somewhat bitter taste and can be picked at any time for culinary use. Dried sage retains its strong flavor and its shape, color and pungent aroma. Harvest no more than one-third of the plant at a time. Use dried branches in wreaths and as an insect repellent.

From ancient times sage has been credited with increasing mental capacities, memory and wisdom. Sage is an Old English word meaning "wise person." *Salvia* is from the Latin meaning "I am well."

Common Sage
S. officinalis
Also called green or garden sage, common sage is a perennial with lilac-colored flowers that grows over 2 ft. and has a tendency to sprawl if not trimmed. After the first year, leaf harvests can be taken twice a season. Dry common sage for seasoning turkey stuffing.

Golden Sage
S.o. 'Icterina'
Because of its variegated yellow and pale green leaves, golden sage is a charming accent plant in the landscape. It also makes a tidy edging or container plant. It has a milder flavor than common sage and can be used for garnishing soups and salads.

Mexican Bush Sage

S. leucantha

Mexican sage has gray-green leaves and spikes of abundant lavender to purple flowers that attract hummingbirds. Growing to a height of 4 ft., it is used more often as a garden accent and as a background plant than in the kitchen. Mexican sage is not winter-hardy.

Purple Sage

S.o. 'Purpurascens'

Use the soft purple-shaded strongly flavored leaves in teas and as a seasoning. In the garden, its unusual color works well combined with plants with dark green or gray leaves. It can be pinched and pruned for dramatic effect.

Pineapple-Scented Sage

S. elegans

The profuse, bright scarlet fall-blooming flowers and attractive leaves of pineapple-scented sage have a distinct pineapple aroma. It is the least hardy of the sages, but it makes a good container plant and can be grown indoors in a sunny window in winter. The leaves have little flavor. Use pineapple-scented sage for garnishing teas and fruit salads and in sachets.

Variegated Sage

S.o. 'Tricolor'

Tricolor is a half-hardy and very decorative variety of sage. Its leaves offer an ever-changing variegation of green, lavender and cream. It makes a lovely accent plant in the garden. When added to recipes, butters and vinegars, it offers a milder flavor than other sages.

SANTOLINA
Santolina species

Santolina is a tender perennial often treated as an annual. It grows well in full sun and well-drained soil. It is cultivated for its aromatic fern-like foliage. Rub the leaves to release the scent. *S. chamaecyparissus*, often called lavender cotton, has gray leaves and yellow flowers, and *S. virens* has dark green leaves and chartreuse flowers.

Because santolina takes to regular pruning, it is a good choice for a low hedge or as an element of a knot garden. It is known to resist drought and tolerate salty soil, making it an excellent seashore plant. Hang dried bunches in closets to repel insects. Use both flowers and leaves in dried floral arrangements.

Good Herbs for Potpourri

Anise
Basil
Bay
Caraway
Chamomile
Cilantro
Hyssop
Lavender
Lemon verbena
Marjoram
Mints
Rosemary
Sage
Santolina
Scented geraniums
Tansy
Thyme

Making Potpourri

First Select an appealing mixture of herb leaves and flowers for size, color and scent. For maximum color and fragrance, harvest on a warm, sunny day and carefully cut half-opened blooms.

Then Air-dry whole flowers by placing them on newspapers in a warm, airy dark spot. Dry flowers still attached to stems by hanging them flower-end down.

Third Dry leaves by pulling off those that aren't wilted or bruised and spreading them on newspapers or screens in a warm, airy, dark place. To preserve color, cover flowers in a box of drying powders, such as silica, or in sand.

Fourth To prevent the evaporation of the oils and hold the fragrance, add a fixative of 1 tbs. chopped orris root, citrus peel, vetiver or storax for each quart of herbs.

Fifth To enhance the aroma or add an accent aroma, purchase and add an essential oil. Consider dividing the potpourri and adding a different oil to each portion.

Last Mix the flowers, leaves, fixative and a touch of essential oil and store in an airtight glass or ceramic container in the dark. Shake or stir the mixture once a week. After a month, transfer the potpourri to gift jars or bags.

Savory
Satureja species

Salt Substitute

Of all the savories, the two best known are summer savory, *S. hortensis*, and winter savory, *S. montana*. Both like full sun and well-drained soil.

Summer savory (below) is a sweet-tasting, highly aromatic annual. It germinates quickly from seed. It makes a good border hedge and indoor or outdoor container plant.

Winter savory (right) is a hardy, semi-evergreen perennial with a stronger aroma than summer savory. Seeds germinate slowly. Allow the soil to dry between waterings. Winter savory makes a compact bush or hedge. Consider it for rock and knot gardens and indoor or outdoor containers.

Harvest savory when it is about six inches tall. To extend the harvest, snip the tops of the branches only. At the end of the growing season, harvest both winter and summer savory by cutting whole plants and drying them, using the air-drying method (see opposite page). The Saxons named it savory for its pungent peppery taste. With its strong flavor, it can be substituted for salt in seasoning blends (see page 31).

DRYING HERBS

The key to proper drying is to reduce the water content as quickly as possible. There are four drying methods: by air circulation; by ovens; by means of drying powders; or by using a dehydrator.

Dry leaves and flowers by means of air circulation. Cut whole stems or branches, brush or wash off the dirt and remove any dead leaves and spent flowers. Label each bundle; tie stems together and place them on newspapers or drying screens or hang them upside down in a dark, well-ventilated room. Hanging works best for flowers. After a few weeks, remove the leaves from the stems.

To dry leaves in a gas or electric oven, snip the leaves off the stems or branches and chop stems and roots into pieces and place them on a baking sheet. Put them in a 150° F oven for a few minutes, leaving the door ajar.

In a microwave, place a single layer of snipped leaves on a paper towel. Set at full power. After one minute, turn the herbs and continue cooking until dry. Watch for burning.

Dry delicate flowers by completely burying them in drying powders or use a dehydrator according to manufacturers' directions.

Prevent mold by making sure leaves, flowers and roots are completely dry before storing them. Dried herbs will retain their shape and color for about a year.

SCENTED GERANIUMS
Pelargonium species

Scented Apple Geraniums
P. odoratissimum
Apple-scented geranium has small, velvety leaves with a very intense apple scent. It has fluffy clusters of white flowers that bloom on vine-like, trailing branches. Use it in hanging baskets and window boxes. Add minced leaves to apple jelly, cider and tea.

Scented Lemon Geraniums
P. crispum
Lemon-scented geranium grows to 3 ft. tall on a slender stem. Its small, crinkled leaves are traditionally used in finger bowls and potpourris. They can be dried in bunches and hung in closets to give clothes a fresh, lemon scent.

AROMATIC WONDERS

Scented geraniums make lovely house and garden plants. Grow scented geraniums for their distinctive fragrances, flavors and colorful leaf patterns. Unlike most plants, it is the leaves, rather than the flowers, that carry the scent. Place plants along borders and paths and near doorways where they can be brushed easily and enjoyed.

Although perennials, scented geraniums are not winter-hardy. Locate them in a protected garden area for seasonal color. In containers near a sunny window indoors, they will thrive year-round.

While they grow rapidly from seed sown in warm, 75° F soil, the plants that result may not be fragrant. Named varieties are best purchased as transplants started by cuttings in spring or summer. Take cuttings at any time and place them directly in damp sand or soil with organic amendments and good drainage. They grow well in full sun, with some shade during the hot summer months.

Let the soil dry completely between waterings to prevent root rot. Fertilize sparingly, unless the foliage becomes weak and pale or there is little new growth. Adding too much fertilizer can make for large, lush growth, but will diminish the leaves' fragrance.

Scented geraniums bloom best when somewhat pot-bound. Pinch their growing tips every few weeks in early growth stages to encourage side branching and bushiness. Remove faded flowers regularly so that the plants will continue to bloom. The flowers are neither aromatic nor flavorful.

Harvest the leaves at any time. Use them fresh or dried.

Scented Lime Geraniums

P. x nervosum

One of the bushier varieties of scented geraniums, lime has an abundance of large, strikingly handsome lavender flowers and attractive toothed leaves. Use the leaves to add a strong lime scent and flavor to desserts and jellies.

Scented Rose Geraniums

P. graveolens

The leaves of rose-scented geraniums are the most fragrant of the scented geraniums. There are several rose-scented geraniums. Use their spicy aroma as a substitute for roses in potpourri. Add them to tea, cakes, cookies, jam and wine.

Scented Peppermint Geraniums

P. tomentosum

The peppermint-scented geraniums have white flowers. Because of its trailing, prostrate growing habit and its large, velvety leaves, this plant is ideal for growing in hanging baskets and containers. Add the leaves, which have a very strong mint aroma, to teas and jelly.

Scented Strawberry Geraniums

P. scabrum

One of the fruitier smelling of the scented geraniums, the strawberry variety will grow to be a large shrub with shiny, crinkly leaves and a charming lavender flower. Add the minced leaves to flavor fruit salads, jellies, desserts and teas.

SOCIETY GARLIC
Tulbaghia violacea

Society garlic is a close relative of true garlic. The edible, star-shaped flowers and the leaves have a mild garlic flavor when crushed or cut. Use the minced leaves for seasoning soups, stews and salads. Use the flowers for garnishing.

A perennial, society garlic is an evergreen in mild climates. It grows well in full sun where its rosy lavender flowers will bloom all summer long. Because its many narrow leaves grow in clumps, the plant makes a beautiful border in beds. One popular selection, with white-margined leaves, is called 'Silver Lace'.

MAKING HERB BUTTER

Herb butter combines available fresh herbs with sweet butter for a flavorful spread. Because sweet butter contains no salt, herb butter is a good low-sodium diet alternative.

Good herbs for making butter include chives, dill, society garlic, watercress, mint, tarragon, lovage, and caraway. Rosemary butter is good on lamb chops. Oregano butter goes well with roast corn. Combined basil and parsley butter works nicely on fish or vegetables. Make a *fines herbes* (see page 51) butter for eggs, French bread or pasta.

RECIPE

To make herb butter combine $1/2$ cup sweet (unsalted) butter, which has been warmed to room temperature, with 3 tablespoons minced *fresh herbs*, 2 minced shallots, 1 tablespoon white wine vinegar and $1/8$ teaspoon of white pepper. Alternatively, use $1 1/2$ teaspoons dried herbs or $1/2$ teaspoon of herb seeds per $1/2$ cup butter. Use less of such strongly flavored herbs as oregano, thyme and society garlic. If the herb is mild, use more.

Place ingredients into a blender or food processor and mix until smooth. Roll the mixture into a cylinder and cover with foil, or place in a covered crock, butter mold or ice cube tray. Refrigerate for three hours until the mixture is firm and the tastes meld. Store in the refrigerator for one week or the freezer for two months.

SORREL
Rumex scutatus

Sorrel, often called French sorrel, is a cultivated member of a wild and weedy perennial family called *dock*. Like other docks, it is difficult to eradicate once it is established. It is best grown in a contained area in a sunny location in well-drained soil. Propagate by seed or by division. Cut back frequently for bushy leaf production.

Harvest sorrel leaves any time. Young and tender leaves are best. Use them fresh for a sour, lemon-like tang in salads and soups. High in vitamin C, sorrel was once employed as a cure for scurvy and as a digestive aid. Dry the flowers for use in arrangements.

FREEZING HERBS

Freezing is an alternative preservation method suitable for many herbs. For herbs including bay laurel, chervil, mint, marjoram, rosemary, sage and thyme, freezing is as good a way of preserving them as drying. For basil, chives, dill, fennel, parsley and tarragon, freezing is a better choice than drying, as the low temperature helps maintain flavors longer. Freeze herbs right after harvesting. Herbs can be frozen for about six months, after which they begin to deteriorate.

To freeze herb leaves, brush or wash soil from the leaves and remove the leaves from plant stems. To retain a strong color, blanch the fresh herbs before freezing. To blanch, place leaves in a strainer and pour boiling water over them. Hold under cold running water to cool. After blanching, cool leaves to room temperature. Some of the taste and fragrance of the herb is lost through blanching. However, some leaves turn black if you don't blanch them.

Put serving-sized amounts, separately or in combinations, into labeled freezer-proof plastic containers and place them in the freezer until needed.

Substitute frozen herbs for fresh herbs in recipes. Throw them directly from the freezer, without defrosting, into soups, stews and sauces. Defrost and drain herbs before adding to uncooked foods.

SWEET WOODRUFF

Galium odoratum

A perennial shade-loving herb, sweet woodruff develops its distinctive scent—similar to new-mown hay—as its whorls of leaves dry. Craft uses include drying for potpourris and as an aromatic filling for herb wreaths and garlands. In Germany, it flavors May wine, a traditional drink to toast the passage of winter and to greet spring. Except for alcoholic beverages, sweet woodruff is not recommended for culinary use.

Grow white flowering sweet woodruff as a rapidly spreading, fragrant ground cover under trees and along paths. Seeds will germinate in the fall; when established it will self-sow freely. Also propagated by division.

KNOT GARDENS

The classic geometric herb garden was a tradition in England during the Middle Ages and Renaissance. In these gardens, complex interwoven patterns were formed with a variety of herbs and surrounded by low hedges and paths. Viewed from above, they resembled the knotted shapes and patterns made by lacemakers and weavers.

Formal, symmetrically designed herb gardens remain popular today. They may or may not have true knots. Any sunny, flat piece of land that can be seen from above is a good candidate for one. Usually at least three varieties of herbs of contrasting foliage color, texture and form are necessary to obtain a pattern. Compact low-growing perennial herbs that tolerate pruning work best. Consider installing hyssop, lavender, lemon thyme, rosemary, sage and santolina. Avoid using such invasive herbs as tansy and catnip.

These gardens can be very simple. Designs based on checkerboards, spokes of a wheel or squares divided into four are fairly easy to lay out. Another option is to create borders that are neat and even, and within these borders to install informal plantings. Consider different decorative effects by planting a particular type of herb within each area, or by installing plants with contrasting foliage, leaf texture and form and flower color.

Measure and lay out the design, using stakes and strings to line up angles and spaces. For interlocking knots, grow plants very close together to effect a continuous strand. Where rows intersect, prune the plants so that the top strand is shaped to look like it flows over the lower strand. Plan the formal garden with space around and between plants to make grooming easier.

Because it needs to be carefully designed, pruned and weeded, establishing and maintaining a formal garden is time consuming, but the effect can be a stunning addition to the home landscape.

TANSY
Tanacetum vulgare

BITTER BUTTONS

Tansy is a tough, easily grown perennial. It produces a three-foot-tall mass of yellow button-shaped petalless flowers in late summer. These become clusters of seedheads that remain on the plant through winter and reseed in spring. Because of the strong pine smell of the small round flowers, tansy is often called bitter buttons.

Tansy thrives in any soil but likes good drainage and maximum sun. It provides attractive foliage and lush growth. Tansy spreads rapidly through runners and can choke out less vigorous plants. To prevent it from getting out of bounds, thin it yearly in spring, or grow it in containers. Placed near a path, tansy will release its woodsy scent each time people brush by.

Its strong smell makes tansy an excellent insect repellent. It is said to help keep ants, moths and flies away when planted around the house foundation or near doorways and windows. It was once used as a strewing herb. Try placing dried sprigs in drawers or closets to repel moths.

In the past, tansy leaves were used in folk medicine and cooking. It may have been the bitter herb in the Passover seder and Lenten recipes. It is now known to irritate the stomach and should not be eaten.

Tansy has many craft uses. It retains its unusual aroma when dried, making it a good selection for potpourri. Its fern-like leaves, pretty flowers and seedheads are long lasting, maintaining both their shape and color for weeks in a dried arrangement, making it perfect for wreaths.

Making an Herb Wreath

First Purchase materials at craft centers. Use a wire base for fresh arrangements, polystyrene for dried. Wrap 24-in. gauge florist's wire around 3 in.–long bunches of bay laurel, santolina or tansy leaves and stems for the background.

Third Wrap fresh or dried tansy and any other contrasting leaves, flowers, pods or berries that are available. Attach clusters with wire as accent material.

Next Starting from the inside, overlap and attach layers of the background herbs in one direction until the base is covered to desired thickness. Arrange leaves to cover stems.

Last Add ribbons, bells and seasonal items for an unusual gift. Hang wreaths on doors and windows. Avoid direct sunlight. Wreaths will dry and fade but can be kept indefinitely.

TARRAGON
Artemisia dracunculus

THE DRAGON HERB

The culinary herb tarragon—specifically, French tarragon—is a perennial with distinctively flavored leaves. Its flowers bloom rarely, and, when they do, they seldom set seed.

Propagate tarragon by cuttings or by dividing in spring. In fact, dividing every three or four years is mandatory to ensure vigor and flavor. The name tarragon comes from the French *estragon,* meaning "little dragon," referring to the roots of the plant, which, if not divided, will strangle the plant eventually.

Tarragon does best in full sun and very well drained, slightly sandy soil. To get two leaf harvests a year, simply cut the leaf stems four inches from the ground, once in late summer and again in late fall. Dry them using the air circulation method.

Tarragon is difficult to grow in very warm climates or where winters are wet. It dies to the ground, is dormant in winter and must have cold and a good protective mulch at that time to grow back in spring. You can grow tarragon year-round by putting it in a container in mid summer—no later—and growing it indoors in a very sunny window.

Primarily, tarragon is a culinary herb. The leaves have a unique flavor and are used in many gourmet recipes, especially in salad dressings and vinegar and on fish. It is one of the *fines herbes* (see page 51) and an important seasoning in rémoulade, bernaise and tartar sauces. Tarragon is strong tasting and should be used with restraint.

Harvest leaves at any time. Tarragon is best fresh, frozen or stored in vinegar; drying destroys some of the unique pungent flavor.

MAKING HERB VINEGAR

A number of herbs lend themselves to flavoring vinegar. Tarragon is the most popularly employed, but basil, bay laurel, chervil, chives, lavender, parsley and thyme are delicious choices as well.

For stronger flavored herbs—basil, bay, tarragon—use a good white-wine or cider vinegar. For milder flavored herbs, use white distilled vinegar.

RECIPE

Sterilize glass or ceramic bottles with lids, to be used in the making, but not the storage, of the herb vinegar. Put ½ cup of cleaned fresh herb leaves or sprigs (or 2 tablespoons of dried herbs) per pint of vinegar in a sterilized container. Bring vinegar to a boil and pour over the herbs to fill the container.

Tightly cover the containers. Set them in a cool, dark place; lightly shake the container daily.

The mixture should be flavored properly after two or three weeks. Strain the vinegar into a sterilized decorative jar or bottle. Small wine bottles are a good choice. Place a sprig in the bottle to identify and decorate the vinegar.

Fit the containers with new corks or rubber or plastic stoppers. Do not use metal caps. Label the bottle. Vinegars should keep indefinitely. However, any home-bottled vinegar that develops a questionable appearance or odor should be discarded.

THYME
Thymus species

THE HERB OF COURAGE

Thyme is a many branched, aromatic perennial shrub grown for its culinary uses. It is a good choice for the beginning gardener. Grow from seeds, transplants, by cuttings taken anytime from mid spring to early summer or by division. It grows vigorously in any well-drained soil. After it is established, thyme requires relatively little care.

All varieties, both upright and trailing, need to be pruned back severely and frequently. Otherwise the plants become woody and scraggly and need to be replaced every two or three years.

Pick thyme leaves as needed. Harvest the entire plant in mid summer by cutting it back almost to the ground. The plant will grow back again before the season is over. If you take a second harvest, the plant will not be able to withstand winter as well. Bees enjoy thyme; if you don't care to have bees around, harvest the leaves before the blossoms open in mid summer.

Thyme is one of the *fines herbes* (see page 51) of French cuisine. Its leaves and sprigs blend well with almost all foods; most recipes can be improved by it. Thyme is traditionally used for garnishing and in clam chowder, *bouquets garnis,* herb butters, seasoning blends and flavored vinegars.

Dried leaves and flowers retain their flavor and aroma well. Preserve via the air circulation drying method or by freezing.

Thyme originated in the Mediterranean, and, over the years, has been the source of legend and lore. The word *thumus* is Greek for courage. In ancient Greece the scent of thyme was assigned to nobility for bravery and the herb was given as a symbol of courage to those who had no fear of death.

Caraway Thyme
T. herba-barona
Good for growing in hanging baskets and as a ground cover, this thyme is a prostrate shrub with rose-colored flowers and arching branches. Use it as a substitute for caraway for flavoring soups, vegetables and poultry.

Common Thyme
T. vulgaris
Common or English thyme is a small, woody, upright shrub. It is one of the herbs in *bouquet garni* and works well as a flavoring in slow-cooked soup stocks and bean and meat dishes. Use fresh common thyme sparingly in recipes as its taste is strong.

Lemon Thyme

T. x citriodorus

A small upright bush with pale pink flowers and strong lemon-scented foliage, lemon thyme makes a great seasoning for fish or chicken. The leaves make a tasty tea and, when dried, an excellent addition to potpourris.

Silver Thyme

T. vulgaris 'Argenteus'

Silver thyme has variegated foliage that is lovely in hanging baskets and as a compact accent plant in garden borders. It can be used interchangeably with English thyme for culinary endeavors. Use its white-edged leaves in floral arrangements and wreaths.

Mother-of-Thyme

T. praecox subspecies *arcticus*

A traditional ground cover, mother-of-thyme is a creeping, tough variety that forms a thick, dense mat. The dark green leaves can be used to season cooked food or dried for use in potpourris.

Woolly Thyme

T. pseudolanuginosus

A vigorous ground cover with tiny rose-pink flowers and tiny silver-gray leaves, woolly thyme is a good choice for planting between stepping stones, in a rock garden or along walkways. It grows readily from seed and will fill in the nooks and crannies of the garden floor, creating a scented leafy carpet.

HERB REFERENCE CHART

HERB	PLANT TYPE			HOW TO START					WHERE TO GROW						EXPOSURE		
	Annual	Perennial	Biennial	Seed Indoors	Seed Outdoors	Transplant	Dividing	Cuttings	Indoors	Container	Ground Cover	Bed	Border	Accent	Sun	Partial Sun	Shade
Anise	•				•	•				•		•		•	•		
Dark Opal Basil	•				•	•						•	•	•	•		
Holy Basil	•				•	•						•			•		
Lemon Basil	•				•	•						•	•		•		
Spicy Globe Basil	•				•	•				•		•	•		•		
Sweet Basil	•				•	•				•		•			•		
Thai Basil	•				•	•						•			•		
Bay Laurel		•				•				•				•	•	•	
Borage	•				•					•	•	•			•		
Caraway			•		•							•			•		
Catnip		•			•		•	•		•	•	•			•		
Dyer's Chamomile		•			•					•		•		•	•	•	
German Chamomile	•				•					•		•			•		
Roman Chamomile		•			•					•	•				•		
Chervil	•				•							•					•
Chives		•			•	•	•		•	•		•	•		•		
Cilantro	•				•					•		•				•	
Peppergrass	•			•	•				•	•							•
Watercress		•						•	•	•						•	
Winter cress			•		•	•		•	•	•							•
Dill	•				•							•			•		
Bronze Fennel		•			•							•		•	•		
Common Fennel		•			•							•			•		
Florence Fennel		•			•							•			•		
Hyssop		•			•		•	•		•	•	•	•		•		
English Lavender		•		•	•	•		•		•		•	•	•	•		
French Lavender		•		•	•	•		•		•		•	•	•	•		
Spanish Lavender		•		•	•	•		•		•		•	•	•	•		
Spike Lavender		•		•	•	•		•		•		•	•	•	•		
Lemon Verbena		•			•	•		•	•	•				•		•	
Lovage		•		•	•	•	•					•		•	•	•	
Apple Mint		•			•		•			•	•	•				•	
Bergamot Mint		•			•		•			•	•	•				•	
Corsican Mint		•			•		•			•	•					•	
Pennyroyal		•			•		•				•					•	
Peppermint		•			•		•			•		•				•	
Pineapple Mint		•			•		•			•		•				•	
Spearmint		•			•		•	•		•		•				•	

SOIL NEED					PLANT HEIGHT				WHAT TO USE					HOW TO USE								PG.
Sand	Clay	Dry	Well-Drained	Moist	Less Than 12"	12"–24"	24"–36"	More Than 36"	Leaves	Stems	Flowers	Seeds	Roots	Not Edible	Eat Fresh	Eat Cooked	For Tea	In Vinegar	For Butters	In Arrangements	For Potpourri	
			•		•				•	•	•	•				•					•	8
			•		•				•							•		•				11
			•		•				•						•					•		10
			•		•				•							•				•		11
			•		•				•						•	•		•				11
			•			•			•						•	•		•				10
			•					•	•						•	•						11
		•	•					•	•					•						•	•	12
			•			•			•		•				•							14
				•	•				•			•	•		•	•				•		16
•				•	•				•					•				•				18
			•			•					•					•			•			21
			•		•						•								•		•	20
			•		•				•										•		•	20
		•		•		•			•						•	•						22
		•			•				•		•				•			•	•	•		24
				•					•	•		•	•		•	•	•					26
				•	•				•						•							28
				•	•				•	•					•					•		28
				•				•	•						•							29
		•					•				•				•	•			•	•		30
	•		•					•	•		•				•	•						33
	•		•					•	•			•	•		•	•						33
			•					•	•						•							33
•			•	•	•						•			•						•	•	34
•		•	•	•			•		•		•					•				•	•	36
•		•	•			•					•					•				•	•	36
•		•	•		•						•					•				•	•	37
		•	•				•				•					•				•	•	37
•			•				•		•						•	•	•				•	38
				•				•	•		•				•	•			•			40
				•		•			•						•		•	•		•	•	42
				•	•				•						•		•	•		•	•	42
				•		•			•						•		•	•		•	•	42
				•	•				•					•							•	43
				•		•			•						•		•		•		•	43
				•					•						•		•	•	•		•	43
				•	•				•						•				•		•	43

HERB REFERENCE CHART (continued)

Herb	Annual	Perennial	Biennial	Seed Indoors	Seed Outdoors	Transplant	Dividing	Cuttings	Indoors	Container	Ground Cover	Bed	Border	Accent	Sun	Partial Sun	Shade
Nasturtium	•			•	•				•	•	•	•			•	•	
Common Oregano		•		•		•	•	•		•	•				•	•	
Crete Dittany		•		•		•	•	•		•			•		•	•	
Italian Oregano		•						•		•		•			•	•	
Golden Oregano		•		•		•	•	•		•	•				•	•	
Sweet Marjoram		•		•	•	•	•	•		•		•			•	•	
Pot Marjoram		•						•		•		•			•	•	
Curly Parsley			•		•				•	•		•	•		•	•	
Italian Parsley			•		•				•	•		•	•		•	•	
Roquette	•				•					•		•					•
Common Rosemary		•				•		•		•		•	•	•	•		
Creeping Rosemary		•				•		•		•	•				•		
Common Sage		•		•		•	•					•	•		•		
Golden Sage		•		•		•	•					•	•	•	•		
Mexican Bush Sage		•		•		•	•					•	•	•	•		
Pineapple-Scented Sage		•		•		•	•		•	•		•	•		•		
Purple Sage		•		•		•	•					•	•		•		
Variegated Sage		•		•		•	•					•	•	•	•		
Santolina		•			•		•	•				•	•		•		
Summer Savory	•				•			•	•	•			•		•		
Winter Savory		•			•		•	•	•	•		•	•		•		
Scented Apple Geranium		•				•		•		•			•		•	•	
Scented Lemon Geranium		•				•		•		•			•		•	•	
Scented Lime Geranium		•				•		•		•			•		•	•	
Scented P. mint Geranium		•				•		•		•	•		•		•	•	
Scented Rose Geranium		•				•		•		•			•		•	•	
Scented S. berry Geranium		•				•		•		•			•		•	•	
Society Garlic		•				•						•	•	•	•		
Sorrel		•			•		•			•		•			•		
Sweet Woodruff		•			•	•	•				•	•	•				•
Tansy		•		•		•	•			•					•		
Tarragon		•					•	•	•	•		•			•	•	
Caraway Thyme		•			•	•	•	•	•	•	•		•		•		
Common Thyme		•			•	•	•	•	•	•		•			•		
Lemon Thyme		•			•	•	•	•	•	•		•			•		
Mother-of-Thyme		•			•	•	•	•	•	•	•				•		
Silver Thyme		•			•	•	•	•	•	•			•	•	•		
Woolly Thyme		•			•	•	•	•	•	•	•				•		

| | SOIL NEED | | | | PLANT HEIGHT | | | | WHAT TO USE | | | | | HOW TO USE | | | | | | | | PG. |
Sand	Clay	Dry	Well-Drained	Moist	Less Than 12"	12"–24"	24"–36"	More Than 36"	Leaves	Stems	Flowers	Seeds	Roots	Not Edible	Eat Fresh	Eat Cooked	For Tea	In Vinegar	For Butters	In Arrangements	For Potpourri	
		•	•		•				•		•	•			•					•		44
		•	•			•			•						•	•				•	•	46
		•	•			•			•						•	•					•	46
		•	•			•			•						•	•					•	47
		•	•		•				•						•	•					•	47
		•	•			•			•						•	•	•	•	•		•	47
		•	•			•			•						•		•		•		•	47
		•		•	•				•	•			•		•	•	•		•			48
		•	•	•	•				•	•					•	•	•					49
				•	•				•	•			•		•	•			•	•		50
•		•					•		•		•				•				•		•	52
•		•			•				•		•				•	•					•	52
•		•					•		•						•	•				•		54
•		•				•			•						•	•				•		54
•		•						•	•						•					•		55
•		•				•			•						•		•				•	55
•		•							•							•	•					55
•		•														•		•	•	•		55
		•				•			•		•				•	•			•		•	56
	•		•		•				•						•	•		•				58
•		•	•		•				•						•	•		•				58
•	•	•	•			•			•		•					•						60
•	•	•	•				•		•		•					•					•	60
•	•	•	•			•			•		•					•						61
•	•	•	•			•			•		•					•	•					61
•	•	•	•			•			•		•					•	•				•	61
•	•	•	•				•		•		•					•	•					61
			•			•			•		•				•					•		62
		•		•		•			•		•				•						•	64
		•		•	•				•	•				•						•	•	66
•	•	•					•		•	•				•						•	•	68
•		•				•			•						•	•		•	•			70
•		•			•				•						•	•		•	•		•	72
•		•			•				•						•	•			•		•	72
•		•			•				•	•					•	•			•		•	73
•		•			•				•						•	•			•		•	73
•		•			•				•	•					•	•		•		•		73
		•			•				•	•					•	•			•		•	73

INDEX

A Note From
NK Lawn & Garden Co.

For more than 100 years, since its
founding in Minneapolis, Minnesota,
NK Lawn & Garden has provided
gardeners with the finest quality seed
and other garden products.

We doubt that our leaders, Jesse E.
Northrup and Preston King, would
recognize their seed company today, but
gardeners everywhere in the U.S. still rely
on NK Lawn & Garden's knowledge and
experience at planting time.

We are pleased to be able to share this
practical experience with you through
this ongoing series of easy-to-use
gardening books.

Here you'll find hundreds of years of
gardening experience distilled into easy-
to-understand text and step-by-step
pictures. Every popular gardening
subject is included.

As you use the information in these
books, we hope you'll also try our lawn
and garden products. They're available
at your local garden retailer.

There's nothing more satisfying than
a successful, beautiful garden. There's
something special about the color of
blooming flowers and the flavor of home-
grown garden vegetables.

We understand how special you feel
about growing things—and NK Lawn &
Garden feels the same way, too. After
all, we've been a friend to gardeners
everywhere since 1884.